Enological studies. I. Experiments in cider making applicable to farm conditions. II. Notes on the use of pure yeasts in white wine making

Alwood, William Bradford

Copyright © BiblioLife, LLC

This historical reproduction is part of a unique project that provides opportunities for readers, educators and researchers by bringing hard-to-find original publications back into print at reasonable prices. Because this and other works are culturally important, we have made them available as part of our commitment to protecting, preserving and promoting the world's literature. These books are in the "public domain" and were digitized and made available in cooperation with libraries, archives, and open source initiatives around the world dedicated to this important mission.

We believe that when we undertake the difficult task of re-creating these works as attractive, readable and affordable books, we further the goal of sharing these works with a global audience, and preserving a vanishing wealth of human knowledge.

Many historical books were originally published in small fonts, which can make them very difficult to read. Accordingly, in order to improve the reading experience of these books, we have created "enlarged print" versions of our books. Because of font size variation in the original books, some of these may not technically qualify as "large print" books, as that term is generally defined; however, we believe these versions provide an overall improved reading experience for many.

Issued November 12, 1909.

U. S. DEPARTMENT OF AGRICULTURE,
BUREAU OF CHEMISTRY—BULLETIN No. 129.
H. W. WILEY, Chief of Bureau.

ENOLOGICAL STUDIES.

I. Experiments in Cider Making Applicable to Farm Conditions.
II. Notes on the Use of Pure Yeasts in Wine Making.

BY

WILLIAM B. ALWOOD,
ENOLOGICAL CHEMIST.

WASHINGTON:
GOVERNMENT PRINTING OFFICE.
1909.

CONTENTS.

	Page.
I. Experiments in cider making applicable to farm conditions.	5
Cider made from low-grade apples in hot weather.	5
Character of raw material.	5
Notes on condition of samples during fermentation.	6
Analyses of bottled ciders.	8
Cider made from winter apples in cold weather.	10
Plan of the experiment.	10
Fermentation notes.	10
Discussion of chemical data.	17
Final notes on the commercial condition of ciders.	19
Ciders of 1907 in bottles as taken from cellar June 1, 1909.	19
Same bottles after standing erect three hours in ice.	19
Note on the vinegar keg.	20
II. Notes on the use of pure yeasts in wine making.	21
Introduction.	21
An experiment on the control of fermentation.	21
Notes on fermentation of three vats of Ives grapes sown with yeast No. 162 (all drawn to cask No. 64).	22
Record of vat 11.	22
Record of vat 3.	23
Record of vat 2.	24
Notes on vats adjacent to Nos. 11, 3, and 2, but neither yeasted nor supervised.	25
Vat 10.	25
Vat 5.	25
Vat 12.	25
Notes on wine cask No. 64 filled from vats 11, 3, and 2.	25
Notes on fermentation of three vats of Ives grapes, not yeasted (all drawn to cask No. 26).	26
Notes on vat 1.	26
Notes on vat 6.	26
Notes on vat 8.	27
Notes on cask No. 26 (containing vats 1, 6, and 8, not yeasted).	27
Comparison of Brix and temperature readings.	28
Analytical data on the samples taken during the progress of the experiment.	30

ILLUSTRATION.

	Page.
Fig. 1. Ventilation funnel.	15

ENOLOGICAL STUDIES.

I. EXPERIMENTS IN CIDER MAKING APPLICABLE TO FARM CONDITIONS.

CIDER MADE FROM LOW-GRADE APPLES IN HOT WEATHER.

CHARACTER OF RAW MATERIAL.

In September, 1906, an experiment in making bottled cider was undertaken at Nehawka, Nebr. That district furnishes a large quantity of fruit of unmerchantable grade which is worked up into vinegar stock, fruit juice, and fermented cider. The fruit is, on the whole, rather low in sugar and therefore better suited for vinegar stock than for either cider making or preserving as unfermented juice. Also the high temperature of September, when most of it must be worked up, renders cider making rather difficult without the construction of cool cellars. This experiment was, however, undertaken with a view to ascertaining what the character of the cider would be when made from this fruit under the ordinary conditions of factory work.

The following analyses show the general character of the fruit grown at Nehawka that year. As these figures are for one year only, it is fair to state that it was a favorable season and probably these results are fully up to the best average composition of these varieties as grown in that district.

TABLE I.—*Analyses of juice of ripe fall and winter apples grown at Nehawka, Nebr.* (*H. C. Gore, analyst*).[a]

[Grams per 100 cc.]

Variety.	Total solids (calculated).	Sugar-free solids (calculated).	Reducing sugar, invert.	Sucrose.	Total sugar, invert.	Acid as malic.
Gano [b]			6.79	3.31	10.27	0.38
York Imperial	12.57	1.45	7.82	2.87	10.84	.43
Black Twig	13.44	1.22	8.89	2.78	11.82	.45
Roman Stem [b]	14.79	1.73	7.64	5.06	12.97	.36
Winesap	14.14	2.35	8.95	2.41	11.49	.43
Rhode Island Greening [c]	11.99	1.30	7.45	2.67	10.26	.57
W. W. Pearmain	12.59	1.45	5.55	5.13	10.95	.46
Grimes Golden [d]	13.19	1.06	7.42	4.43	12.08	.28
Fameuse [e]	13.89	2.18	8.87	2.50	11.50	.34
Jonathan [e]	13.74	1.52	9.65	2.17	11.93	.40
Ben Davis [b]	e 12.02	.48	7.50	3.56	11.25	.48
Average	13.24	1.48	7.87	3.35	11.40	.42

[a] J. Amer. Chem. Soc., 1907, 29:1112.
[b] Mealy.
[c] Slightly mealy and somewhat withered.
[d] Slightly withered.
[e] Average of 10 determinations.

The average sugar content of these varieties is 11.40 per cent, about 1 per cent below the general average of our best American apples, and the juice on which the experiment was made was even poorer, as shown by the following determinations, also made by Mr. Gore: Specific gravity, 1.0497; total sugar, 10.15 per cent; total acid as malic, 0.287 gram per 100 cc. Frequently specific-gravity readings of the juice as expressed at the cider mill at Nehawka were as low as 1.045, and the acid was quite uniformly low. The fruit used for the experiment was mixed, but was chiefly Grimes Golden.

NOTES ON CONDITION OF SAMPLES DURING FERMENTATION.

On September 4, 1906, juice from the mill having at 71° F. a specific gravity of 1.045 was put into flasks and sterilized by boiling fifteen minutes in a water bath. This was cooled, and at 11 a. m. four pint flasks were sown with yeast, one each with Nos. 8, 53, 66, and 73, respectively.[a] These were put in the rooms having a temperature of 70.7° F.

September 5.—Fermentation commenced in the flasks sown with yeast. Temperature of fermentation room, 72° F.

September 7, 7 a. m.—All flasks have fermented strongly, and heavy foam rests on the surface, except No. 66, which is bare, and foam is breaking up on No. 8. Fermentation room, 79° F. all day.

September 8.—Fermentation room 74° F. at 7 a. m.; 80° F. at 5 p. m.

September 10, 8 a. m.—Fermentation room 76° F.

September 11, 8 a. m.—Fermentation room at 78° F. Weather has been very warm, temperature running up to from 95° to 98° in the shade each day.

September 12, 8 a. m.—Fermentation room 66° F. Rained and turned cooler.

September 13.—Fermentation room 60° F. at 8.30 a. m. Filled four 30-gallon barrels with fresh must and sowed at 11 a. m. with yeasts Nos. 8, 53, 66, and 73, as before, 1 pint of each culture being used. Room temperature was 66° F., juice temperature 62.6° F. in barrels. Marked each cask with number of yeast used in it. Cask No. 8, specific gravity 1.048; No. 53, 1.049; No. 66, 1.049; and No. 73, 1.049.

This juice is chemical sample No. 55 of Mr. Gore's notes, and the differences in specific gravity are explained by the fact that his determinations were made on a pyknometer and those here given on a spindle.

5 p. m.—Fermentation room 68° F.

---

[a] On application to Wm. B. Alwood, Stonehenge laboratories, Charlottesville, Va., a circular giving further details in regard to these yeasts may be obtained.

EXPERIMENTS APPLICABLE TO FARM CONDITIONS.

September 14, 8 a. m.—Fermentation room 68° F., juice 64.5° F. in all casks. No. 8 in strong fermentation, head forming and extinguishes match. No. 53, same as No. 8. No. 66 fermenting slowly. No. 73 same as No. 66.

5 p. m.—Fermentation room 68° F.

September 15.—Fermentation room at 8 a. m., 70° F. Barrel No. 8 shows loose, coarse dark foam, temperature 69° F.; No. 53 shows dark foam, temperature 69° F.; No. 66 shows coarse light foam, temperature 69.8° F.; and No. 73 shows coarse light foam, temperature 69.8° F.

All in strong fermentation. Specific gravity, Nos. 53 and 66, 1.045. Readings were not made on the other barrels.

5 p. m.—Temperature of fermenting room, 76° F. Storing hot bottles of sterilized juice in this room has caused rise of temperature.

September 16, 8.30 a. m.—Fermentation room 74° F. Barrels Nos. 8 and 53 show head loose, frothy, disappearing; temperature 73.4° F.; Nos. 66 and 73 show almost no head, temperature 74° F. Specific gravity Nos. 8 and 66, 1.039. Readings were not made on the other barrels.

September 17, 8 a. m.—Fermentation room 74° F. Barrels Nos. 8 and 53 show a temperature of 76° F.; Nos. 66 and 73, temperature 77° F. Foam on all barrels had disappeared.

September 18.—Fermentation room 72° F. Cider in all casks shows temperature of 76° F.; all quiet, did not take specific gravity.

September 19.—Fermentation room 70° F. The casks all show a temperature of 75.2° F. Specific gravity of barrel No. 8, 1.024; No. 53, 1.023; No. 66, 1.024; No. 73, 1.021.

September 20.—All are quiet, color of cider ocherous, cloudy. Fermentation room 70° F. Temperature in all casks, 73.4° F. No. 8 is still fermenting and frothy when drawn. Nos. 53, 66, and 73 are all quiet and without foam when drawn; color pale opalescent, fermenting slowly.

September 21.—Fermentation room 70° F. Temperature in all casks 73° F.

September 22.—Fermentation room 70° F. Temperature in all casks 71.6° F. Specific gravity of barrel No. 8, 1.012; No. 53, 1.011; No. 66, 1.013; and No. 73, 1.010. None have precipitated yeasts as much as they should have.

10 a. m.—Racked off a 15-gallon cask from each barrel and left them in the fermenting room; all samples very opalescent and not settled. The original barrels were bunged and left in position, not full.

September 24.—Fermentation room 68° F. All the racked ciders are still fermenting and still opalescent; No. 8 decidedly active. No. 73, specific gravity 1.006, others not taken.

8 ENOLOGICAL STUDIES.

September 25.—Fermentation room 68° F. No. 8 specific gravity in the original barrel, 1.002, the color is opalescent. The remnant was run through a milk separator, which brightened it decidedly, showed a specific gravity of 1.002 at temperature of 69° F. No. 8 in sample racked September 22, shows a specific gravity of 1.007, the racking checked fermentation decidedly.

Bottled 18 quarts from the original barrel for samples. No. 53, original barrel, shows a specific gravity of 1.001, at a temperature of 69.8° F.; color opalescent. This was run through the milk separator and gave a specific gravity of 1.001, on completion at temperature 69.8° F came out bright. The sample racked in keg shows a specific gravity of 1.006. Bottled 18 quarts of cider from the original barrel.

No. 66, original barrel, shows a specific gravity of 1.002, temperature; 69.8° F., liquid opalescent. This was run through a separator, also, and cleared markedly; specific gravity 1.002 at completion. All of these numbers taste much alike after being run through the separator; they are of a pale straw color and translucent in glass, not exactly bright.

Bottled 18 quarts from original barrel No. 66, the sample racked on September 22, shows a specific gravity of 1.006.

No. 73, original barrel, has a specific gravity of 1.000, temperature 69.8° F., quiet, dull straw color, clearer than the others. Separator used as in other cases. Specific gravity remains at 1.000.

Bottled 18 quarts from original barrel of No. 73. The keg that was racked on September 22 showed a specific gravity of 1.004. Of the preceding four samples about 30 gallons were run through the separator without cleaning the machine and then a large amount of very compact viscous, slimy sediment was found on its walls. Removed nearly one-half pint of this heavy greenish slime.

September 26.—Samples from each number, after passing through the separator, were put in the ice box and at 8 a. m. on this date tasted very flat, were nongaseous and almost characterless, No. 66 being the most agreeable and No. 73 quite dry. All are free from bad tastes and odors. The ciders direct from the barrels are fairly good in quality, sprightly foam, not rich. No. 73 racked into keg shows a specific gravity of 1.0038, others not taken.

ANALYSES OF BOTTLED CIDERS.

The writer left Nehawka on September 27, and Mr. H. C. Gore, assistant chemist in the Bureau of Chemistry, bottled the samples racked into kegs as noted above without further notes on condition.

On September 29 Nos. 53 and 73 were bottled and on October 1, Nos. 8 and 66 were bottled. Analyses as given in Table II were made of all these ciders at bottling. These samples were taken to the Bureau of Chemistry and held in storage until the following April, when a final analysis was made, as given in Table III.

TABLE II.—*Analyses of cider made at Nehawka, Nebr., 1906 (H. C. Gore).*

FERMENTED AND RACKED TO KEGS.

Bureau of Chemistry serial number.	Yeast number.	Date of analysis.	Specific gravity.	Alcohol (per cent by weight).	Invert sugar (grams per 100 cc).	Acid as malic (grams per 100 cc).
86	8	October 1.....	1.0011	5.02	0.57	0.218
84	53	September 29..	1.0007	4.90	.68	.191
87	66	October 1.....	1.0015	5.02	.59	.205
85	73	September 29..	1.0003	5.04	.50	.191

FERMENTED IN ORIGINAL BARREL.

75	8	September 25..	1.0007	4.82	0.57	0.205
76	53	....do........	1.0006	4.95	.56	.205
77	66	....do........	1.0006	4.73	.75	.177
78	73	....do........	1.0004	4.95	.38	.244

TABLE III.—*Final analyses of the cider made at Nehawka, Nebr. (H. C. Gore).*

RACKED FROM BARRELS INTO KEGS SEPTEMBER 22; ANALYZED APRIL 11, 1907. (QUITE WELL GASSED.)

Bureau of Chemistry serial number.	Yeast number.	Date of bottling (1906).	Specific gravity.	Alcohol (per 100 cc).	Reducing sugar (per 100 cc).	Solids (calculated) (per 100 cc).	Acid as malic (per 100 cc).
				Grams.	*Grams.*	*Grams.*	*Grams.*
17827	8	October 1.....	0.9984	5.14	0.11	1.91	0.39
17828	53	September 29..	.9984	5.16	.08	1.87	.40
17829	66	October 1.....	.9989	5.08	.15	1.93	.44
17830	73	September 29..	.9983	5.26	.08	1.84	.43

SAMPLES FROM ORIGINAL BARRELS PASSED THROUGH MILK SEPARATOR; ANALYZED APRIL 17, 1907. (VERY SLIGHTLY GASSED.)

17848	8	September 25..	1.0014	4.96	0.60	2.44	0.36
17849	53	....do........	.9999	5.05	.41	2.11	.38
17850	66	....do........	1.0012	4.88	.61	2.40	.38
17851	73	....do........	.9993	5.07	.27	2.02	.42

At the date of analysis as given in the table the ciders bottled from the juice racked into kegs from the original barrels were sufficiently gassed to pour with a fine foam, and though light in color and weak in flavor they were very good ciders. Those bottles which were filled from the original barrels after the juice had been clarified by passing through a milk separator were but slightly gassed. This difference is largely due to the removal of much of the yeast by the process of clarification.

The chemical data given for the time of bottling and for the final examination show decidedly that the samples which were passed through the separator retained the sugar content almost without change, while those samples racked and bottled without clarification fermented almost entirely dry.

The unclarified ciders were decidedly superior in pleasantness of flavor, due largely to the carbon dioxid gas present. This examination appears to suggest, however, an interesting point—that possibly clarification by use of a separator and bottling direct without exposure to contamination might enable one to hold ciders of low alcohol content and containing considerable unfermented sugar.

Considering the character of the fruit used, these ciders were of superior quality. The method of handling is certainly simple, especially with those that were racked as indicated and bottled a few days later.

CIDER MADE FROM WINTER APPLES IN COLD WEATHER.

PLAN OF THE EXPERIMENT.

The following notes give in detail the operation of making cider in the simplest possible manner after cold weather begins These notes, taken as the work progressed, are presented in sufficient detail to make plain every operation. The work was intended to approximate as closely as possible the conditions under which a farmer might ferment his cider for family use, and the results establish clearly a method which any person of ordinary means can use. The plan of the experiment comprised simply the use of two pure cultures of yeast in comparison with a check cask left to natural fermentation.

FERMENTATION NOTES.

October 23, 1907.—Crushed and pressed 60 bushels of Winesap apples. The fruit was of a grade called unmerchantable, but was not rotten nor soiled. From the fresh juice three 50-gallon whisky barrels were filled for the experiment and a 10-gallon keg was left untreated and unnumbered beside the barrels. No. 1 was left to natural fermentation, No. 2 sown with yeast No. 73 (Sauternes), and No. 3 sown with yeast No. 161 (Ahrweiler). The juice from the vat at the mill tested 1.055 on the specific gravity spindle, corresponding to a Brix reading of 13.6°. The color and flavor were very good.

The barrels used were secondhand whisky barrels, and were steamed for twenty minutes with live steam from the boiler, then rinsed with clean water and drained, and one-half pint of 90 per cent alcohol was poured into each, after which they were tightly bunged and laid in the storeroom, where they remained two weeks before use.

The casks were not sulphured, but were filled direct at the mill and the yeast cultures added at once. The cultures are made by inoculating 400 cc (approximately 1 pint) of sterilized apple juice with the yeast desired, three days before it was needed, and it was in full fermentation when used. The barrels were replaced in the storeroom, which is above a basement, the walls being of boards slatted on one side, so that it is dry and airy. The wooden bungs were removed and the barrels plugged with cotton. It has since developed that cotton plugs are not safe to use in barrels with fermenting juice, because if the cotton becomes the least bit damp, malferments readily find entrance to the must.

October 24, 4 p.m.—Temperature of juice in all casks is alike, 13°C., approximately 56.7° F., and the reading on the specific-gravity spindle is the same as before, 1.055. There is no appearance of fermentation. The weather has turned sharply cold for the season and the room is cold.

October 26.—No. 1 is still, No. 2 is foaming at bung, and No. 3 shows foam on liquor.

October 29.—No. 1 remains quiet, temperature 9° C., approximately 48° F., Brix 14.1°; No. 2 more quiet, foam subsided, temperature 9° C., Brix 13.9°; No. 3 less active, temperature 9° C., Brix 14°. Room temperature 11° C., approximately 52° F., at 4 p. m.

Microscopic examination made with the following results:

No. 1: Few yeast cells present, but more cells of Torulæ. Tastes exactly the same as fresh juice.

No. 2: Yeasts are fairly plentiful; no Torulæ seen; Apiculatus present; foam thrown up is mostly composed of yeast cells; taste piquant.

No. 3: Yeast cells present as in No. 2, but do not find Apiculatus or Torulæ; foam largely yeast cells distinguishable from those of No. 2; tastes about like No. 2; less fermentation.

October 30, 4 p. m.—Room temperature 10° C., approximately 50° F. No. 1 remains unchanged; No. 2 has again thrown foam out at bung; No. 3 has thrown foam out at bung. The temperature rises at about noon, but is so cold at night that proper fermentation can not develop in this room.

October 31.—The outdoor temperature fell last night to freezing, and this morning the experimental cider casks were moved to the inner cellar of the laboratory, where the temperature is practically constant at from 13° to 14° C., approximately 55.4° to 57.2° F. The temperature of liquors Nos. 1, 2, and 3 is 9° C., 48.2° F.; Brix 14.1° for No. 1, and for Nos. 2 and 3, 13.7°. Taste of No. 1 entirely sweet, others fermenting; flavor fine.

November 1.—No. 1 shows slight activity. Nos. 2 and 3 fermenting calmly. Placed ventilating funnels on all barrels, but the small keg of the same juice was left with cotton plug.

November 2.—No. 1 is now very active; pushed mass of foam out through ventilating apparatus. This foam, unlike Nos. 2 and 3, contains but few yeast cells. Nos. 2 and 3 fermenting calmly; no overflow of foam.

November 4.—Microscopic examination: No. 1 shows a large number of true yeast cells, some having peculiar long forms. Torulæ are also present, but no Apiculatus or Mycoderma; fermenting quietly.

No. 2 shows true yeast dominant; Torulæ are also present; no Apiculatus or Mycoderma; fermenting calmly.

No. 3 has but few yeast cells in the liquor and none of the malferments; fermenting calmly. Yeast No. 161 used in No. 3 is a highly coagulated yeast and falls rapidly to the bottom. Already this characteristic is plainly shown by the clear appearance of the liquor.

November 5.—Nos. 1, 2, and 3, temperature of liquor 15° C. (59° F.) and a Brix of 11.8°, 11.1°, and 11.7°, respectively. None has yet cleared.

November 16.—All are fermenting calmly.

November 19.—All are progressing with apparently sound fermentation.

December 9.—All of the barrels are in good condition; very quiet; no head or foam on liquor. Brix readings as follows: No. 1, Brix 7.3°, specific gravity 1.029; No. 2, Brix 5.8°, specific gravity 1.023; No. 3, Brix 6.8°, specific gravity 1.027, all on Westphal balance at 15° C; temperature in barrels 12° C.

Nos. 1 and 2 are in very good condition, but the liquor is pearly opalescent in color, while No. 3 is decidedly brighter—so much so that persons unfamiliar with the character of such liquors note it at once.

The flavor of all the samples is good, but No. 3 is milder and more agreeable. Only a slight difference between Nos. 1 and 2.

While the barrels showed foam on the surface at times, no characteristic "head" was formed, and it was decided not to rack the liquor off until it had reached about the conditions observed in handling wine—that is, after the liquor had become practically bright and free from sediment.

December 24.—The small 10-gallon keg left with only a cotton plug in the bung has not been noted until to-day and now has a decided flavor of vinegar. This will be carried along with the cider barrels to observe the progress of this sample in acetic fermentation.

January 10, 1908.—For some time past the temperature in this cellar has been purposely lowered by opening a small window, and it has been running from 9° to 12° C. (approximately 48.2° to 53.6° F.). This morning, after a very cold night, it is at 6° C. (42.8° F.), the lowest point reached. The window was closed. Temperature of liquor in all barrels is 10° C. (50° F.). Brix readings: No. 1, Brix 5.7°, specific gravity 1.0225; No. 2, Brix 3.1°, specific gravity 1.012; and No. 3, Brix 4.6°, specific gravity 1.018; all on Westphal balance at 15° C.

No. 1 has suffered in activity by this low temperature and shows scarcely enough carbon dioxid over the surface of the liquor to extinguish a match, while Nos. 2 and 3 extinguish a match promptly. Color of Nos. 1 and 2 about the same, dull straw, not bright; No. 3 clear and bright. The bouquet is similar for all, but the flavor is distinctly different, which is partly accounted for by the difference in sugar content; yet there is an after tang to No. 1 which is not desirable. No. 2 is noticeably more agreeable and free from this taste. No. 3 has a clear, mild, fine flavor, fruity and pleasant without aftertaste. All are promising.

The microscopic examination shows the liquor in all barrels to be almost free from organisms of every kind. No. 1 shows a few yeast cells and there are now a few Mycoderma cells and Torulæ present. No. 2 shows a very few small cells not characteristic of yeast. No. 3 showed no material in suspension.

Six pint bottles were filled from each barrel to observe the fermentation as it might develop in glass, corked with champagne corks, tied, and laid in the cellar.

January 13.—The 10-gallon keg shows a cover of vinegar ferment which forms a firm skin on the surface; specific gravity 1.010, Brix 2.6°; is quite bright and of fine quality considered as a vinegar sample. Microscopic examination of sample does not show any organisms floating in the liquor.

Racked off all of the cider to-day, temperature 10° C. (50° F.) in all the casks. Used for receptacles whisky barrels of same descriptions as for Nos. 2 and 3, and a 25-gallon cask for No. 1.

These were cleaned and stored as in the previous case, but before using were washed with warm water and sulphured, using one-third of a sulphur match. This sulphured the casks to saturation, or consumed all the air. The cider was poured in on the sulphur fumes. In this work the ciders are handled both with and without the use of sulphur for the purpose of securing experimental data.

No. 3 was drawn first and proved to be of a bright amber color, limpid and clear. The cider was drawn off down to within 1 inch of the bottom of the barrel and was poured through a funnel covered with a thin woven laboratory towel and left almost no show of dregs. Brix 4.3°, specific gravity 1.017 at 15° C. The quality was superb for a new cider. About 2 quarts of dregs remained in the barrel, of a dirty greenish color, slightly gelatinous but not pasty like wine lees.

No. 2 was next drawn and came off opalescent in color, slightly clouded in lower portion, showed decided dregs on towel in funnel. The dregs left in the barrel were about like those of No. 3, but were not gelatinous. This cider does not equal No. 3 in brightness by many points, but the quality is good. It has fermented more than

No. 3 and now reads Brix 3°, specific gravity 1.011 at a temperature of 15° C. (59° F.).

No. 1 was racked last. It was similar in color to No. 2, but too sweet to compare flavors. This cider is promising, but the wild yeasts have not been able to ferment the sugar in the low temperature maintained recently. Brix reads 5.7°, specific gravity 1.022, temperature 15° C. (approximately 59° F.). The dregs from No. 1 were thin and did not show nearly so much sediment as Nos. 2 and 3.

Four gallons of No. 1. were used to fill up No. 3 and 5 gallons to fill up No. 2. The remainder of No. 1 was put in quart bottles to be used in filling up wantage.

January 15.—The temperature of the cellar is 10° C. (50° F.). Since racking there has been very little or no fermentation in the barrels. The temperature of the cellar is carried low purposely, but so far as noted the temperature in the barrels has not fallen below 10° C. (50° F.).

January 17, 7 a. m.—Some slight fermentation in barrels Nos. 1 and 2. *8 a. m:* Gas is passing slowly from No. 1; *4 p. m:* Removed 50 cc from Nos. 1 and 2, both showed in stem of funnel but had not overflowed.

January 19.—Changed bung on No. 1 and put in short bung because of overflow.

January 21.—Took bottled stock from cask No. 1, filtered and bottled 2 dozen pints. Specific gravity before filtering was 1.022 on Westphal balance, and after filtering the same. The cider was dull yellowish amber to straw color; only two quart bottles could be put through one paper with any speed, after that it was most tedious work until a new filter paper was put in. Corked with champagne corks and then heated in water to 70° C. (158° F.) for ten minutes, two bottles left unheated, marked, and cork tied down. Stored all in inner cellar. Two corks blew out in second run of sterilizer; fourteen bottles sterilized, two bottles not sterilized.

January 22.—Was obliged to take long bung out of barrel No 2 to prevent overflow.

January 27.—Took out all long bungs, filled casks Nos. 1 and 2, bored the bungs crosswise to let out the gas, and then put in the long bungs again with vent funnels. (See fig. 1.)

This bung and ventilating device as here shown permits the escape of gas, when the cask is entirely full of liquor, by means of the cross orifice.

January 28.—Temperature of cider in barrels is 11° C. (51.8° F.).

January 30.—From this date the temperature of cellar was maintained at 11° C. to 14° C. (51.8° to 57.2° F.).

February 14.—All barrels passing gas slowly.

February 18.—Same.

February 25.—No. 1 is much more active than others.

February 26.—No. 1, temperature in barrels 13.5° C. (56° F.), specific gravity 1.019; Nos. 2 and 3, 14° C. (57.2° F.), specific gravity 1.008 and 1.0145, respectively, by Westphal balance at 15° C. (59° F.). (Cask No. 1 is smaller than others, hence is cooler.)

Bouquet of all faint but agreeable; flavor varies because of sugar present, but No. 1 still has an unpleasant aftertaste, though less than formerly. It is a good cider. No. 2 is much dryer than No. 1, very good, clear, and sound. No. 3 has a fine flavor, no aftertaste. Color of Nos. 1 and 2 similar. No. 3 is pale straw, almost bright, resembling a young Rhine wine. These samples are all that could be expected in a good cider.

February 27.—All ciders analyzed for the first time. (See Table IV, p. 18.)

February 29.—Analyzed the 10-gallon keg turned to vinegar. This is now in fine condition and promises to be good vinegar; specific gravity 1.009.

March 16.—Samples bottled on January 10, 1908, noted as follows:

No. 1 in strong fermentation, two bottles show slight leaks. Throws cork instantly when tie is cut, pours over frothy, liquor cloudy, bouquet fair, flavor good, but unpleasant aftertaste remains, acidity good, sound.

No. 2, almost bright in bottle, slight sediment deposited, no pressure, but shows slight bead when poured, limpid, clear, almost bright, bouquet good, flavor excellent, color clear rich straw amber, acidity good, fine cider.

FIG. 1.—Ventilation funnel. *a*, glass ventilating device; *b*, long wooden bung; *c*, longitudinal orifice; *d*, diagonal cross orifice; *e*, perforated cork on stem of ventilating device. (See also Bul. 111, Bureau of Chemistry, p. 8.)

No. 3, almost bright in bottle, noticeable sediment which is dark, no pressure, less bead when poured than No. 2, slightly paler in color and a bit more bright, bouquet good, flavor excellent, extra good quality, acidity good, sound.

March 18.—Analyzed bottled samples, but results are not given in table, as they were practically identical with the results for the original barrels as analyzed March 20.

March 20.—Analyzed the samples in barrels. (See Table IV, p. 18.)

April 15.—Nos. 1 and 3 discharge gas slowly; No. 2 so still that seldom shows escape of gas.

April 17.—Examined ciders Nos. 1, 2, and 3. All have now become clear and practically the same brightness, condition fine, show some gas in liquor, are approaching each other in aroma and flavor. Specific gravity on No. 1, 1.012, Brix 3.1°; No. 2, 1.010, Brix 2.6°; and No. 3, 1.011, Brix 2.9°, Westphal balance at 15° C. (59° F.). Apparent discrepancy in reading of No. 2 on this date, compared with February 26, must be due to inaccuracy of previous reading.

May 5.—Cider No. 1, filtered, bottled, and sterilized January 21, 1908, is clear and bright, fine amber color, sediment very compact on side of bottle. Opens perfectly still, flavor sweetish without character, rather unpleasant aftertaste, aroma stale, not desirable. Specific gravity 1.021.

Bottle of same date not sterilized shows very light flocculent matter all through liquor, lees not deposited to any extent, liquor paler than No. 1 but not bright, looks badly in bottle. Opens with high pressure, foamed over, deposit rushed out with liquor, fairly good color, not bright, heavy foam in the glass; flavor good but with an undesirable aftertaste; aroma strong, fruity. Specific gravity 1.017.

June 22.—All casks passing gas, No. 1 as before, but Nos. 2 and 3 very slowly.

June 25.—Began final bottling of the ciders.

No. 1, specific gravity 1.006 at 15° C. (59° F.), Brix 1.6°, liquor is quite highly charged with gas, color opalescent, dull straw amber, but no visible particles, aroma slightly rank, like that of fungus growth. Flavor, good, fruity, not delicate, aftertaste still slightly unpleasant, not easily defined, but less agreeable than Nos. 2 and 3. Drew about two-thirds of the cask direct into bottles, then filtered the remainder bright; lost all gas in filtering. This is a promising cider. Marked No. 1A and No. 1B.

No. 2, specific gravity 1.008 at 15° C. (59° F.), Brix 2.1°; liquor is not charged with gas like No. 1, but is saturated. Color about like No. 1, possibly a trifle brighter. Aroma good, clear, fruity, no smell of fungus; flavor clear, delicate, finely acid, agreeable. Bottled about two-thirds of a barrel direct, retaining gas.

Filtered remnant, barely enough to cover the large asbestos filter used, but got it through fairly bright, lost all gas. This is a very good cider. Marked No. 2A and No. 2B.

No. 3, specific gravity 1.006 at 15° C. (59° F.), Brix 1.6°. Liquor not charged, but fairly saturated with gas. Color a decided shade brighter than Nos. 1 and 2, aroma delicate, neutral; flavor sprightly, delicate, neutral, very good, no aftertaste. Finest cider ever handled here. Bottled about two-thirds direct and ran remnant over the filter as in case of No. 2; but there was not enough to secure the best results. It bottled retaining more gas than the others. Refiltered last por-

EXPERIMENTS APPLICABLE TO FARM CONDITIONS. 17

tion over a small asbestos filter, very bright. Almost no lees remained in these casks. Marked No. 3A, No. 3B, and No. 3B special.

All of these ciders were placed in pint champagne bottles and left in the large workroom to observe the start of fermentation.

July 16.—Removed all bottled cider from workroom to cellar No. 1. Unfiltered ciders show a slight deposit, but no gas on opening bottle. Filtered ciders show in some cases a very slight deposit, much less than before. The quality of these ciders is very good. Cellar temperature 20° C. (68° F.).

November 2.—Sample No. 34, 10-gallon keg which turned to vinegar, racked off and put into jugs, one small jug corked tight and held in cellar as sample for further study.

DISCUSSION OF CHEMICAL DATA.

The chemical data presented in Table IV cover the examination of the original apple juice and give a full series of analyses of the several casks of cider and vinegar as the fermentation progressed, in the case of the first three to cider and in the fourth to vinegar.

The first analysis of the several samples of cider on February 27, 1908, shows conclusively that up to this time the yeasted packages had fermented more rapidly than the unyeasted ones, yeast No. 73 giving about 1 per cent the most alcohol. From this date, however, until the last analysis was made on March 3, 1909, this yeast slackened decidedly, and the unyeasted casks gradually passed it in attenuation of sugar, exceeding also yeast No. 161.

But it is a most interesting point that, considering the alcohol produced for sugar consumed, yeast No. 161 has surpassed both yeast No. 73 and the natural fermentation; and if the present alcoholic strength of these ciders be increased by the possible alcohol which could theoretically be formed if these ciders were fermented entirely dry, yeast No. 161 would still show an excess of alcohol of 0.3 per cent over yeast No. 73 and of 0.5 per cent over the natural fermentation. The analyses have been most carefully checked, and hence are used with confidence.

The fact that cider No. 2 retains such a considerable quantity of sugar after the lapse of eighteen months is very important. It is now, on June 1, 1909, the best cider of the experiment, being many points superior to No. 1 and noticeably better than No. 3.

The condition of these ciders as to content of volatile acid shows that they are perfectly sound; however, No. 1, natural fermentation, shows a greater amount of volatile acid than the others. The total acid in all the samples is about right for a sprightly cider—namely, approximately 0.40 per cent.

18 ENOLOGICAL STUDIES.

TABLE IV.—*Chemical data on cider and vinegar made from winesap apples.* (*Hartmann, Eoff, and Woodson, analysts.*)

Laboratory number	Cider number	Description	Date received	Date analyzed	Specific gravity.	Alcohol.		Sugar (grams per 100 cc).			Acids (grams per 100 cc).				Solids (grams per 100 cc) (calculated).		
						Grams per 100 cc.	Volume, per cent.	Reducing	Sucrose.	Total as invert.	Fixed as malic	Volatile as acetic.	Total as malic.	Total.	Sugar-free.
10		Original apple juice			1.0558	0.129	0.161	11.00	0.936	12.02	0.642	0.011	0.654	16.32	3.30
30	1	Plain cider unyeasted	Oct. 23,1907	Feb. 18,1908	1.0183	3.64	4.58	4.72	.010	4.73	.295	.053	.354	6.46	1.73
30	1	...do...	Feb. 27,1908	Feb. 27,1908	1.0158	4.22	5.31	3.82	.057	3.88	.282	.072	.362	6.05	2.17
30	1	...do...	Mar. 20,1908	Mar. 20,1908	1.0108	4.42	5.58	2.77	.038	2.81	.296	.077	.382	4.83	2.02
30A	1A	Not filtered when bottled	Apr. 25,1908	Apr. 25,1908	1.0074	4.06	6.08	1.99	.067	2.00	.324	.094	.429	4.13	2.07
30B	1B	Filtered when bottled	June 24,1908	June 24,1908	a1.0045	5.06	6.38	1.79	.038	1.84	.273	.113	.399		
30A	1A	Not filtered when bottled	Oct. 22,1908	Oct. 22,1908	1.0056	5.12	6.45	1.62		1.70	.265	.114	.392		2.18
30B	1B	Filtered when bottled	...do...	...do...	1.0066	5.02	6.33	1.79		1.79	.286	.106	.405	3.80	2.21
30B	1B	Filtered when bottled	May 3,1909	Mar. 3,1909								.100	.392	4.00	
31	2	Yeasted with No. 73	Feb. 27,1908	Feb. 27,1908	1.0107	4.80	6.08	2.83		2.83	.273	.070	.351	4.83	2.00
31	2	...do...	Mar. 20,1908	Mar. 20,1908	1.0101	4.67	5.88	2.85		2.85	.253	.075	.338	4.76	2.01
31	2	...do...	Apr. 25,1908	Apr. 25,1908	1.0099	4.70	5.93	2.74	.057	2.80	.288	.066	.372	4.73	1.93
31	2	...do...	June 24,1908	June 24,1908	1.0095	4.89	6.17	2.68		2.68	.302	.078	.389	4.63	1.95
31A	2A	Not filtered when bottled	Oct. 22,1908	Oct. 22,1908	a1.0000	4.83	6.08	2.61	.048	2.50	.229	.092	.332	.44	
31B	2B	Filtered when bottled	...do...	...do...	1.0000	4.92	6.20	2.50		2.50	.224	.097	.332		
31A	2A	Not filtered when bottled	Mar. 3,1909	Mar. 3,1909	a1.0084	4.06	6.17	2.36		2.36	.246	.100	.353		
31B	2B	Filtered when bottled	...do...	...do...	1.0083	3.89		2.32		2.32	.250	.100	.362		
32	3	Yeasted with No. 161	Feb. 27,1908	Feb. 27,1908	1.0156	3.86	4.87	4.12	.010	4.13	.304	.038	.346	5.84	1.71
32	3	...do...	Mar. 20,1908	Mar. 20,1908	1.0147	4.57	5.77	3.74		3.74	.257	.065	.330	5.94	2.20
32	3	...do...	Apr. 25,1908	Apr. 25,1908	1.0104	4.80	6.05	2.87	.010	2.88	.269	.071	.348	4.88	2.00
32	3	...do...	June 24,1908	June 24,1908	1.0075	5.26	6.63	2.19	.029	2.22	.272	.092	.375	4.34	2.12
32A	3A	Not filtered when bottled	Oct. 22,1908	Oct. 22,1908	a1.0035	5.43	6.84	2.03	.048	2.04	.251	.096	.358		
32B	3B	Filtered when bottled	...do...	...do...	1.0030	5.47	6.88	1.80	.010	1.85	.244	.102	.382		
32A	3A	Not filtered when bottled	Mar. 3,1909	Mar. 3,1909	1.0000	4.43	5.58	1.91		1.91	.273	.097	.382	4.63	2.12
32B	3B	Filtered when bottled	...do...	...do...	1.0048	3.55		1.59		1.59	.280	.098	.389	3.77	2.18
34		Fermented to vinegar	Feb. 29,1908	Mar. 1,1908	1.0080	3.81	4.80	1.66		1.66	.444	.883	.346	c1.28	
34		...do...	Apr. 3,1908	Apr. 3,1908	1.0088	3.47	4.37	1.47		1.47	.748	1.238	.330	1.91	
34		...do...	May 15,1908	May 15,1908	1.0105	2.42	3.05	1.25	.038	1.29	.194	2.34	.348	2.72	
34		...do...	June 24,1908	June 24,1908	1.0125	2.00	2.40	1.00	.028	1.11	.223	3.70	.375	3.00	
34		...do...	July 27,1908	July 27,1908	a1.0205	1.14	1.44	1.07		1.27	.246	4.94	.358	5.16	1.67
34		...do...	Nov. 2,1908	Nov. 2,1908								7.02	.123	7.13	
34		...do...	May 26,1909	May 26,1909	b1.0220			1.13		1.13	.080	7.066	.128	1.79	

a Gravity taken on Westphal balance. *b* Gravity taken by pyknometer. *c* This and the subsequent figures are stated as acetic.

EXPERIMENTS APPLICABLE TO FARM CONDITIONS.   19

The alcoholic content of these beverages is high enough for a plain cider, though many commercial ciders are made which contain more alcohol. It appears that it would be very desirable in the future if the alcoholic strength could be limited not to exceed 6 or 6.5 volume per cent and still produce a sound, bright cider of good quality. The special work with yeasts and methods of handling now in progress lead one to believe that this may be accomplished in a practicable manner in the near future.

FINAL NOTES ON THE COMMERCIAL CONDITION OF CIDERS.

The following notes give the commercial condition of these ciders at this time:

CIDERS OF 1907 IN BOTTLE AS TAKEN FROM CELLAR, JUNE 1, 1909

1A. Cider is bright above the sediment. Much deposit spread out over lower surface of bottle, is easily disturbed, light, and floats in masses. All bottles were laid flat in the cellar.

1B. Very bright in bottle, small line of sediment looks like pure yeast, and is not easily disturbed.

2A. Cider is bright in bottle with only moderate deposit, fairly compact, but disturbs easily and floats in small masses.

2B. Cider is bright in bottle, but shows nearly as much sediment as 2A, does not break up quite so readily, floats like 2A.

3A. Cider is bright and fine in bottle, widespread thin layer of film-like deposit, pale colored, breaks readily in films and flakes and floats lightly.

3B. Cider is bright and fine in bottle, deposit far less than 3A, but same character.

There is a marked difference to the eye in the character of the sediment in these different ciders.

SAME BOTTLES AFTER STANDING ERECT THREE HOURS IN ICE.

1A. Sediment all down, slight gas on opening, pours with slight evanescent bead, color pale opalescent; aroma pronounced, not pleasant, characteristic of hard cider. Flavor neither pleasant nor smooth, but characteristic of a hard cider. Quality in general fine for a dry hard cider, but has really lost the fine quality of its flavor noted heretofore.

1B. Sediment all down, bright and clean, opens perfectly still, pours still. Color, clear pale amber; aroma, faint, agreeable; flavor much milder and more agreeable than 1A. Is now decidedly superior to 1A.

2A. Sediment not all down, but is bright and clear in bottle, opens still, pours still, but shows slight gas as it warms in glass; color, very pale amber; aroma, faint, agreeable, fruity.; flavor, mild, agreeable, not wholly dry and not quite so good as heretofore, but an excellent cider.

2B. Sediment not all down, pours still, quite clear and bright, no gas in glass. Color and other points as for 1A, in quality a little smoother in flavor, but less piquant.

3A. Sediment almost all down, bright and clear in bottle, opens with a trifle gas, pours with noticeable bead; color, pale amber, clear; aroma stronger than 2A. Flavor shows a tang of lees, which is not desirable; but this is a good cider.

3B Sediment not all down, but is clear, opens still, pours with barely perceptible gas; color as 3A. Aroma faint, good; flavor smooth, free from tang noticed in 3A. Very good cider, but not equal to 2A and 2B. (The word "clear" means not muddy, nor dirty in color.)

NOTE ON THE VINEGAR KEG.

The small keg No. 34 which was allowed to go to vinegar has yielded an interesting record, which is presented in this connection because the contents formed a part of the original stock used in the experiment and was kept with the other packages until it became vinegar. The first analysis made of this sample gave 3.81 grams of alcohol, 1.66 grams of sugar, and 1 28 grams of total acid, all on a basis of 100 cc. of the sample. It is reasonably accurate to consider these figures as percentages. Comparing these figures with the data for the first three analyses, namely, ciders Nos 1, 2, and 3, it will be seen that the fermentation of the sugar had proceeded much more rapidly in the small keg than in the 50-gallon barrels. This keg was not yeasted, and it is hardly possible to account for the rapid fermentation entirely on the basis of the smaller bulk. Nor is it safe to say without further investigation that alcoholic and acetic fermentation, working together, has stimulated, during the first stage of fermentation, the more rapid destruction of the sugar, but this is indicated.

This more rapid rate of breaking up the sugar does not, however, hold for the subsequent period. In fact during the past fifteen months, while the ciders have fermented in the case of No. 1, 3.11 per cent, of No. 2, 0.5 per cent, and of No. 3, 2.22 per cent of sugar, the vinegar sample has lost but 0.53 per cent of sugar. The loss of sugar in the vinegar sample has been so slight for six months past that it is evident the acid content has now inhibited further yeast action. The complete oxidation of the alcohol to vinegar at the low temperature of this cellar in twelve months is interesting. The fermentation of vinegar in casks in a cool cellar is usually a slow process and often fails or stops before the process is finished. This sample, however, produced a finished vinegar of a very high quality in a year. The total acid, 7 13 per cent, is remarkably strong for such conditions and comes fully up to the total theoretic amount of acetic acid which can be produced from the amount of sugar in the fresh juice.

II. NOTES ON THE USE OF PURE YEASTS IN WINE MAKING.

INTRODUCTION.

The use of pure yeast cultures in the fermentation of wines has three main advantages:

(1) To control the fermentation; that is, by using a sufficient quantity of a strong yeast culture poured onto the crushed pulp in the case of red wine, or into the juice as it runs from the press in the case of white wine, to produce a dominant fermentation with the pure yeast and thereby suppress undesirable wild yeasts and other ferments which injure the quality of the product.

(2) To expedite the process of fermentation and thereby aid in definite direction and control of the fermentation room.

(3) If yeasts are properly selected they may be adapted to develop the special qualities of a must and thereby enable the manufacturer to maintain a better standard of his products.

Rather extravagant claims have been made as to what may be expected from the use of pure yeasts, but the consensus of informed opinion warrants only the statements just made. A pure yeast does not add to a must qualities which it did not originally possess, nor can one possibly hope to imitate particular wines by the use of yeasts selected from those wines. On the other hand, pure yeast cultures well selected for definite regions and for certain types of grapes, if properly used, will greatly aid in producing the best wine that the district is capable of growing and in maintaining the standard of quality. Nothing more can be claimed for them. Yet this is so important that it is safe to predict that the use of pure yeasts will ultimately be the rule. Their use is especially important for the small grower who works for the highest quality and is willing to develop his wines to maturity.

AN EXPERIMENT ON THE CONTROL OF FERMENTATION.

The details of an experiment conducted on a practical scale in the season of 1908 is herein given for the purpose of bringing these definite data to the attention of wine growers. It is not possible at this time to say more about the quality of the product than is said in the general note on the character of the young wine; but as regards the control of fermentation and the facilitating of the work in the vat room, the data presented are complete. The presentation of these notes at this time should serve in a measure as a guide in the details of using yeasts and thereby answer a practical purpose, though a full report on the development of the wines when treated with pure yeasts can not be made until the work now in progress is completed.

The present report comprises the records of two series of vats, one series of which was yeasted with a fresh culture known in this laboratory as No. 162. It was obtained from a good German wine made in the Ahr Valley, and isolated at the Geisenheim laboratories. This yeast was selected because the conditions of wine making in the Ahr Valley bear a resemblance to the conditions in the northern grape belt of the United States, in that the climate is often too cool and the grapes are frequently low in sugar and high in acid.

The yeast cultures were made in 5-gallon bottles of sterilized red grape juice and used when in full activity. The unyeasted vats were handled in every particular like the ones yeasted, save that the yeast culture was not used. One of the vats in this second series, No. 8, was not washed clear of yeast sediment from the former run, but this yeast seems to have given it no advantage over the others of the series. The quantity of native yeast remaining in this vat was equal to many times the quantity introduced by inoculation of the yeasted vats.

This work was done at a winery in Sandusky, Ohio, under the same conditions in every particular as are generally observed at that plant. Each vat was gallized, as described hereafter, in accordance with the practice of the wine maker in these cellars. It should be stated that in describing how this wine was gallized the department does not indorse nor in any way countenance this practice. We merely adopted for the purpose of the experiment the existing commercial practice in order to study the changes wrought by the introduction of the pure yeasts. The work of the author consisted merely in adding the yeast, keeping notes on the progress of the work, and taking the necessary samples for the chemical analyses.

NOTES ON FERMENTATION OF THREE VATS OF IVES GRAPES SOWN WITH YEAST NO. 162 (ALL DRAWN TO CASK 64).

RECORD OF VAT 11.

October 1, 1908, 9.45 a. m.—Yeasted bottom of clean vat with 1.5 gallons of yeast No. 162. Filled with crushed and stemmed Ives. Temperature of pulp 17° C. at start; when half full yeasted again with 1.5 gallons of No. 162. Temperature of pulp 16° C. when half full. Finished filling at 10.20 a. m., used 2.5 tons of fruit; temperature over surface of vat varies from 14° to 16° C.; room temperature 18.6° C.

Gallized, using 125 gallons of sugar sirup made by using 3 pounds of granulated sugar per gallon of water; temperature of sirup 17.4° C.,

Brix 27. This sugar solution showed on analysis 27.08 per cent of pure cane sugar.

11 a. m.: The vat was stirred before sugaring and showed a temperature of 15.4° C., Brix 16.9; sugared and stirred one-half hour; sample 16 finished at 12 m. Temperature 15.4° C., Brix 20.3; yeasted top with about 2 gallons of yeast No. 162; took sample, covered.

4 p. m.: Vat temperature 16.4° C.

October 2, 8.30 a. m.—Vat room 17.4° C.; pulp stirred; temperature 16.8° C.; slight appearance of activity.

10.20 a. m.: Vat temperature 17° C.; slight activity.

2 p. m.: Vat room 20° C.; temperature in vat 17° C.

October 3, 8 a. m.—Vat room 16.7° C.; vat temperature 19° C., Brix 18.6; fermenting evenly.

2 p. m.: Temperature of vat 19° C.; pulp risen, dry, heavy odor of carbon dioxid.

5 p. m.: Temperature 22.4° C., Brix 15.1.

October 4, 7.30 a. m.—Temperature of room 16° C.; in vat 25° C., Brix 8.9.

10.40 a. m.: Drew off vat 11.

Sample 41, free run, temperature 29.4° C., Brix 7.

1 p. m.: Sample 42; took last sample of free run; temperature in vat 28.8° C.; temperature in cylinder 24.6° C., Brix 6.5.

4 p. m.: Sample 43, press wine, temperature 26.8° C., Brix 4.3.

Sample 44, composite of pomace, triturated with mercuric chlorid and bottled for analysis.

Vat room 17° to 20° C. during the day. This vat stood 3 days and 55 minutes on pulp.

October 5.—Pomace of this vat laid on press over night; drainings read temperature 20.6° C., Brix 2. Weight of pomace when taken from press was 1,061 pounds; temperature 28° C.

10 a. m.: Vat room 21.4° C.

Vat 11 was drawn to cask 64 in cellar.

All of the samples taken during this work, both of the fresh juice, the young wine, and the pomace, were preserved with mercuric chlorid and sent to the Stonehenge laboratories at Charlottesville for analysis.

RECORD OF VAT 3.

October 1, 1908, 2.30 p. m.—Yeasted bottom of clean vat with yeast No. 162, filled with crushed and stemmed Ives, using 2.5 tons. Yeasted again when half full. Temperature at start 17° C.; when half full, 17.2° C.; full, 17.2° C.; finished at 3 p. m. Yeasted surface, using in all 3 gallons of very active yeast.

Sample 17: Gallized with 125 gallons of 3-pound sirup, stirred one-half hour; took sample.

3.30 p. m.: Temperature 17.2° C., Brix 16.8; must viscous, not easy to make satisfactory reading on the spindle; covered vat.

October 2, 8.30 a. m.—Vat not stirred; temperature 17° C.

10.20 a. m.: Stirred, temperature 18° C.; slight fermentation.

2 p. m.: Vat room 20° C.; pulp, 18° C.

October 3, 8 a. m.—Temperature 21° C., Brix 17.4; fermenting evenly but more active than vat 11.

2 p. m.: Temperature 21.7° C., fermenting with more visible action than No. 11, but not heating so much.

5 p. m.: Temperature 23.6° C., Brix 13.5.

October 4, 7.30 a. m.—Temperature 27° C., Brix 7.

10 a. m.: Drew off to cask No. 64; free run temperature 30.8° C., Brix 5.4. This vat stood two days, nineteen hours, and thirty minutes on the pulp.

Sample 37: Free run when about one-half off; flavor good, neutral; odor not strong but characteristic.

Sample 38: Last run of vat, temperature 24.4° C., Brix 5.2.

Sample 39: Press wine, temperature 24.8° C., Brix 3.9.

Sample 40: Pomace. Took composite sample and treated with mercuric chlorid and bottled; weight of pomace 1,305 pounds.

RECORD OF VAT 2

October 2, 1908, 8.40 a. m.—Ground and yeasted with 3 gallons of active yeast No. 162, 2.5 tons of Ives grapes.

The pulp ran into vat at 14.5° C.; finished grinding about 9.15, when not well stirred, read Brix 14. Gallized with 125 gallons of 3-pound sirup. Stirred well; done at 9.45 a. m.

Sample 23: Temperature in vat 17° C., Brix 15.7; must is viscous and unsatisfactory; can not read Brix correctly; possibly too many shriveled grapes were used.

October 3, 8 a. m.—Temperature 16.4° C., Brix 16.5; very slight activity.

2 p. m.: Pulp 16.4° C.; slight activity.

5 p. m.: Temperature 17.6° C., Brix 21.2; fermenting slowly.

October 4, 7.30 a. m.—Temperature 18° C., Brix 21.6; fermenting slowly.

4 p. m.: Temperature 21.4° C., Brix 16; fermenting smoothly.

October 5, 7 a. m.—Temperature 24.6° C., Brix 10.4; in fine condition.

11 a. m.: Sample 48. Drew vat, first of free run; temperature 26.6° C., Brix 9. This vat stood three days, two hours, and twenty minutes on pulp.

Sample 49: Last of free run, temperature 26.2° C., Brix 9.1.

Sample 51: Press wine, 2 p. m., temperature 26.6° C., Brix 6.7.

Sample 52: Pomace. Sample taken, treated with mercuric chlorid and bottled. Weight of pomace 1,360 pounds. Wine run to cask 64, holding 1,300 gallons.

NOTES ON VATS ADJACENT TO NOS. 11, 3, AND 2, BUT NEITHER YEASTED NOR SUPERVISED.

VAT 10.

September 29, 1908.—Filled with 2.5 tons of Ives grapes, gallized with 125 gallons of 3-pound sirup.
October 1, 4 p. m.—Temperature 32° C.; no other note made. This is the highest reading noted in the winery in vats filled with Ives.

VAT 5.

September 30, 1908, 7.30 a. m.—Filled with 2.5 tons of Ives grapes; gallized with 125 gallons of 3-pound sirup; not yeasted. No observation on temperature or Brix at filling.
October 4, 9.30 a. m.—The manager was intending to draw this vat, as the crop is crowding the space. Made reading, temperature 23.5° C., Brix 11.4. Advised that it stand longer.
October 5, 8 a. m.—Temperature 27.8° C., Brix 4.7; vat drawn at this time. Total time on pulp five days.

VAT 12.

September 30, 1908, 7 a. m.—Filled with 2.5 tons of Ives grapes; gallized with 125 gallons of 3-pound sirup; not yeasted.
October 4, 7 a. m.—Drew this vat; temperature 21° C., Brix 14.5. Noticed that the pomace was fermenting so strongly that it could not be pressed dry and it took all day to get it off the press. This vat stood on pulp four days.

These notes show the desirability of better control of the fermentation and also the importance of determinations being made to decide when a wine is ready to draw from the pulp.

NOTES ON WINE CASK NO. 64, FILLED FROM VATS 11, 3, AND 2.

October 9, 1908, 11 a. m.—Cask No. 64 is quite still, wine warm, 25.2° C, Brix below zero.
October 10.—Temperature in cask No. 64, 24° C., Brix below zero. Drew 31 gallons for Bureau of Chemistry sample in a 25-gallon and a 6-gallon keg.
December 30.—Sample from cask 64, 25-gallon keg. Wine shrunk about 1.5 inches, covered with flowers, reduces flame at once but does not extinguish match promptly. Drew off clean and almost bright. Aroma fine, strong Ives, flavor smooth, pleasant, very promising; showed considerable gas in wine.
Drew 20 gallons from the 25-gallon keg, then drew two 1-gallon jugs from the 5-gallon keg. The wine was brighter in the latter case. Marked all No. 64.
February 23, 1909.—Wine reached cellar at Stonehenge. laboratories.
March 8.—Ives', cask No. 64.*q!* Color brightest red wine in this lot, aroma good, flavor less acid than some but astringent, good, promising.

26 ENOLOGICAL STUDIES.

NOTES ON FERMENTATION OF THREE VATS OF IVES GRAPES, NOT YEASTED. (ALL DRAWN TO CASK NO. 26.)

NOTES ON VAT 1.

October 2, 1908, 11.30 a. m.—Filled vat 1 with crushed and stemmed Ives, using 2.5 tons. Vat was washed clean; not yeasted. Sample pressed by hand; temperature 14.8°C., Brix, before sugaring, 14.5; must viscous, can not read accurately. Gallized with 125 gallons of 3-pound sirup.

Sample 25: Stirred, took sample. Temperature of sugared must 14.8°C., Brix 16.8.

October 3, 9.30 a. m.—Temperature of vat 14.8° C., Brix 19.6. This seemed to be not well mixed and very sugary.

2.30 p. m.: Temperature 15° C.; not active.

5.30 p. m.: Temperature 16.6° C., Brix 24.5, not active.

October 4, 7.30 a. m.—Temperature 16.6° C., Brix 24.5, quiet.

4.30 p. m.: Temperature 18.4° C., Brix 23.3, quiet.

October 5, 7.30 a. m.—Temperature 19.2° C., Brix 20.2.

4 p. m.: Temperature 19.4° C., Brix 19.4, quiet.

October 6, 7.30 a. m.—Vat drawn; temperature 22.4° C., Brix 13.7. Sample 53, free run.

Last of free run, temperature 22.4° C., Brix 11.2; no sample taken.

Sample 54: Press wine, temperature 23.8° C., Brix 9.5.

Sample 55: Pomace sample treated with mercuric chlorid.

October 6, 7 a. m.—Vat room temperature 21° C.

Vat 1 was drawn too soon; pomace was so frothy that it was difficult to press and the temperature rose while on the press, which should not occur. Weight of pomace was 1,302 pounds, and it was so wet that when barreled the wine ran over the floor. This vat fermented on the pulp three days and twenty hours.

NOTES ON VAT 6.

October 2, 1908, 3 p. m.—Filled with 2.5 tons of Ives; vat washed clean; not yeasted; the fruit was much wilted.

Sample 26: Temperature of pulp 14°C., Brix 16.6; must so viscous it can not be read properly. Gallized with 125 gallons of 3-pound sirup, stirred, Brix 18.8.

October 3, 9.30 a. m.—Vat temperature 15.2° C., Brix 24.2; very sugary, not well mixed.

5.30 p. m.: Temperature 17.2° C., Brix 25.2.

October 4, 7.30 a. m.—Temperature 17.4° C., Brix 25.1, quiet.

5 p. m.: Temperature 18.4° C., Brix 23.8, quiet.

October 5, 7.30 a. m.—Temperature 18.6° C., Brix 21.6, fermenting quietly.

4 p. m.: Temperature 19.2° C., Brix 20.7.

THE USE OF PURE YEASTS IN WINE MAKING. 27

October 6, 7.30 a. m.—Temperature 22.3° C., Brix 16, drawn at 11.30 a. m.

Sample 59: Free run, temperature 24.4° C., Brix 13.8.

1 p. m.: Last free run temperature 25.6° C., Brix 10.1.

Sample 60: Press wine, temperature 25° C., Brix 9, at 3 p. m.

Sample 61: Pomace sampled and treated with mercuric chlorid.

This vat fermented on pulp three days, twenty hours, and thirty minutes.

NOTES ON VAT 8.

October 2, 1908, 1.30 p. m.—Filled with 2.5 tons of Ives. The pulp was run in on yeast from former fermentation. The vat had just been emptied, but not washed; temperature of pulp 14° C., Brix 17.4; vat room 20° C. Gallized with 125 gallons of 3-pound sirup; stirred.

October 3, 9.30 a. m.—Vat temperature 16° C.; temperature of sample in cylinder 17.4° C., Brix 18. Seems to be very sugary.

5.30 p. m.: Vat temperature 17.6° C., Brix 24.4, quiet.

October 4, 7 a. m.—Temperature of vat 17.8° C., Brix 24.4.

5 p. m.: Temperature 18.4° C., Brix 22; foaming a little, particularly at sides; surface uneven.

October 5, 7.30 a. m.—Temperature 19° C., Brix 18.3.

4 p. m.: Temperature 22° C., Brix 15.8; fermenting quietly.

October 6, 7.30 a. m.—Temperature 25.5° C., Brix 10.6; drawn at 9.30 a. m.

Sample 56: Last free run; temperature 26° C., Brix 7.3.

Sample 57: Press wine; temperature 26° C., Brix 6.4.

Sample 58: Pomace sampled and treated with mercuric chlorid.

This vat fermented on pulp three days, twenty hours, and thirty minutes.

NOTES ON CASK NO. 26. (CONTAINING VATS 1, 6, AND 8, NOT YEASTED.)

October 7, 1908, 5 p. m.—Was full; temperature 27.2° C., Brix below zero.

October 10, 4 p. m.—Temperature 26.5° C., Brix below zero; fermenting strongly.

December 30.—Cask not yet racked. Drew off a 32-gallon keg; wine ran off clean and bright; aroma good, characteristic Ives; acidity good; flavor smooth; a sound, promising wine; foamed heavily as it ran from the hose.

February 23, 1909.—Wine reached department cellars at Stonehenge laboratories, Charlottesville.

March 8.—Color fairly bright, aroma fainter than other Ives, but good; flavor fairly smooth and promising, but not equal to cask No. 64, yeasted product.

COMPARISON OF BRIX AND TEMPERATURE READINGS.

For the purpose of more ready comparison, certain of the temperature and Brix readings on each vat are brought together in Table I. In arranging this table the readings of temperature and Brix made each morning have been arbitrarily chosen in the belief that these are more properly comparable than any other readings made. While the periods were not exactly twenty-four hours each, they represent the conditions observed in a manner readily comprehensible and useful to the wine maker. Unfortunately, the condition and character of the grapes used were such as to greatly mar the value of the Brix or gravity readings on the freshly crushed and sugared must. The grapes were so withered in some cases that the juice was viscous and the spindle could not act properly. By an oversight, the Brix readings were not made on vats 11 and 3 on the morning of the second day. But the reading on vat 2 was made, and this, with the readings for the next morning, show the unreliability of these observations. The very striking aberrations of the Brix readings of vats 1, 6, and 8 for the first three observations further show that for this experiment none of the Brix readings had any value until after the wine was in full fermentation, thus bringing about a correction of its viscosity by the action of the alcohol formed All of the first Brix readings except for vat 11 are undoubtedly too low. This reading corresponds fairly well with the sugar and solids found on analysis; and it is further certain that the readings made later, wherein vats 1, 6, and 8 are recorded at 24.5, 24 4, and 25, are too high. The analyses of the finished product do not furnish data to support these readings. Thus it will be plain to practical workers that the use of a spindle for determining the richness of a must has its limitations. In other words, some grapes, and especially wilted Ives, ground and pressed in the ordinary manner, may give a must which can not be read on a gravity spindle. Hence to judge these musts accurately the sample must be prepared so as to obviate this difficulty or the wine maker may be greatly misled.

In this connection it is well to call attention to data obtained on a large number of samples of Ives which were selected so as to fairly represent the normal crop, crushed by hand, and pressed through a cheese cloth bag. This method gave Brix readings sufficiently accurate for all practical purposes

A further observation that bears upon this question is that the stirring of these vats was not adequately done before taking the first sample. While the workmen did the best they could with the bar "stomper" usually employed to mix the mass in the vats, the results of the analyses prove that the mixing was not well done. While this error does not affect the result so far as the fermentation of the wine is concerned, it does very materially affect the character of a sample taken and might mislead. Therefore these discrepancies are important, as observations made under these circumstances might readily lead to error if one is dependent wholly upon spindle readings.

Barring these evident inaccuracies, resulting from conditions which the observer could neither remedy nor control, the table brings together the salient facts of the duration and progress of the fermentation. The Brix readings can be depended upon to show the attenuation after the vats came into full fermentation.

All of the yeasted vats show a marked uniformity of behavior as to rise of temperature and the attenuation of the must so as to bring it into condition for drawing off in a given number of hours. An even progress on the unyeasted vats is also shown, but the attenuation is much slower, and, though these vats were actually drawn after about twenty-four hours' longer period on the pulp than the yeasted vats, two of them were plainly not ready to draw, and foamed so much on the press that they were handled with difficulty.

The sum of the observed temperatures of the respective vats, or, in other words, the total increment of temperature, is interesting. While these observations are not sufficiently accurate as to periods of duration, etc., to warrant the development of a critical argument, they do have a comparative value. The unyeasted vats, for the total time they stood, show a temperature increment in excess of the others, and if they had been carried to the same attenuation as the yeasted vats this excess would have been more noticeable still. It is true that none of the unyeasted vats reached an elevation of temperature within 5° of the yeasted ones, yet if they had completed the tumultuous fermentation they would surely have equaled the others in the degree of heat developed. The highest temperatures noted in this winery were produced in vats undergoing natural fermentation.

TABLE I.—*Comparison of temperature and Brix readings on yeasted and unyeasted vats.*

Data.	Cask 64; all yeasted with No. 162; average time on pulp, 2 days, 23 hours, 35 minutes; average Brix of wine when drawn, 7.13.						Cask 26; not yeasted; average time on pulp, 3 days, 20 hours, 20 minutes; average Brix of wine when drawn, 12.7.					
	Vat 11.		Vat 3.		Vat 2.		Vat 1.		Vat 8.		Vat 6.	
	Temperature.	Brix.	Temperature.	Brix.	Temperature.	Brix.	Temperature.	Brix.	Temperature.	Brix.	Temperature.	Brix.
	°C.		°C.		°C.		°C.		°C.		°C.	
Reading when filled	15.4	20.3	17.2	16.8	17	15.7	14.8	16.8	17	17.4	14	16.6
Reading after 1 day	17		18		16.4	16.5	14.8	19.6	16	18	15.2	24.2
Reading after 2 days	19	18.6	21	17.4	18	21.6	16.8	24.5	17.8	24.4	17.4	25.1
Reading after 3 days	25	8.9	27	7	24.6	10.4	19.2	20.2	19	18.3	18.6	21.6
Reading on fourth day							22.4	13.7	25.5	10.6	22.3	16
Reading when drawn	29.4	7	30.8	5.4	26.6	9	22.4	13.7	25.5	10.6	24.4	13.8
Total of temperature.	105.8		114.0		102.6		110.4		120.8		111.9	

30 ENOLOGICAL STUDIES.

TABLE I.—*Comparison of temperature and Brix readings on yeasted and unyeasted vats—Continued.*

Cask and vat.	Time filled.	Time drawn	Total time on pulp
Cask 64.			
Vat 11	October 1, 9.45 a. m	October 4, 10 40 a. m	3 days, 55 minutes.
Vat 3	October 1, 2 30 p m	October 4, 10 a m	2 days, 19 hours, 30 minutes.
Vat 2	October 2, 8 40 a m	October 5, 11 a m	3 days, 2 hours, 20 minutes
Cask 26:			
Vat 1	October 2, 11 30 a m	October 6, 7 30 a. m	3 days, 20 hours
Vat 8	October 2, 1.30 p. m	October 6, 9.30 a. m	3 days, 20 hours, 30 minutes
Vat 6	October 2, 3 p. m	October 6, 11 30 a. m	Do

TABLE II.—*Chemical data on young wine (Hartmann and Eoff, analysts).*

CASK 64 (IVES) YEASTED.

[Grams per 100 cc.]

Serial No	Field No	Vat No	Specific gravity	Alcohol.	Reducing sugar	Acid			Solids a		Remarks
						Total.	Volatile.	Fixed.	Total.	Sugar-free	
257	16	11	1.0819		19.36	0.469	0.006	0.461	21.28	1.92	Fresh sugared must.
258	17	3	1.0719		16.70	.611	.004	.606	18.66	1.96	Do
427	23	2	1.0660	0.34	15.18	.544	.012	.529	17.27	2.09	Do
421	41	11	1.0267	5.92	6.86	.623	.013	.607	9.57	2.71	Free run from fermenting vat.
424	37	3	1.0205	5.92	8.33	.724	.013	.708	7.97	2.64	Do
428	48	2	1.0254	4.72	8.87	.626	.010	.613	11.34	2.47	Do
423	43	11	1.0153	6.75	3.71	.788	.013	.772	6.95	3.24	Press wine.
426	39	3	1.0139	6.19	3.20	.926	.010	.913	6.38	3.18	Do
430	51	2	1.0260	5.20	5.86	.806	.012	.791	9.10	3.24	Do.
364	44	11		4.74	2.05	1.455	.014	1.437			Pomace.
363	40	3		.25	1.92	.782	.013	.766			Do
366	52	2		1.78	3.58	1.215	.019	1.191			Do.
357	180		.99640	8.77	.302	.679	.024	.649	2.84	2.54	Young wine, Oct 24 1908
473			.99658	8.77	.297	.739	.058	.666	2.89	2.89	Young wine, Mar 8, 1909

CASK 26 (IVES). UNYEASTED

386	25	1	1.0693	0.18	15.88	0.551	0.005	0.545	18.06	2.18	Fresh sugared must.
392	26	6	1.0769	.12	18.16	.420	.006	.412	20.02	1.86	Do
389	27	8	1.0670	.06	15.60	.386	.005	.380	17.41	1.81	Do
387	53	1	1.0565	2.43	12.79	.716	.012	.701	15.81	3.02	Free run from fermenting vat
	59	6	Lost.								
390	56	8	1.0287	4.92	6.42	.818	.005	.812	9.70	3.28	Do.
388	54	1	1.0378	3.70	8.23	.848	.007	.839	11.52	3.29	Press wine.
393	60	6	1.0364	4.58	8.33	.788	.008	.778	11.55	3.22	Do
391	57	8	1.0265	5.24	5.56	.896	.010	.883	9.26	3.70	Do
367	55	1		2.74	8.99		.014				Pomace.
369	61	6		5.12	1.36	1.365	.016	1.345			Do
368	58	8		4.42	1.76	1.260	.019	1.236			Do.
348	169		Lost.	Lost.	2.91	.634	.022	.606	2.66	2.37	Young wine, Oct. 24, 1908.
470			.99540	9.22	.318	.664	.058	.591	2.71	2.42	Young wine, Mar. 8, 1909

a Calculated.

ANALYTICAL DATA ON THE SAMPLES TAKEN DURING THE PROGRESS OF THE EXPERIMENT.

When each vat was filled, gallized, and stirred a sample was taken to represent the unfermented grape juice plus sugar water. From observations made as the experiment progressed, and from the analyses of the young wines as drawn and of the wines in each of the casks when completed. it is conclusively shown that these samples of

THE USE OF PURE YEASTS IN WINE MAKING. 31

the fresh sugared must did not represent the material in the vats with accuracy. This is especially true of vats 1, 6, and 8, but in case of vats 11, 3, and 2 the fresh samples more nearly represent the material. This is pointed out also in the preceding section. It is therefore necessary to disregard the results of the analyses of the samples of the fresh material and confine the discussion to the data furnished by the samples of the young wine as drawn from the vats and the samples of the wines from the casks.

The discrepancy due to unequal sampling is perhaps greatest in the case of the sugar content, but other constituents would doubtless be affected in a lesser degree. It is evident, from the analyses of the young wines, that the average sugar content of the material fermented for cask 64, yeasted, must have been about 18 per cent, while by the same reasoning that for cask 26, unyeasted, must have contained quite 19 per cent sugar. Eliminating, therefore, the analyses which were made of the samples of the freshly sugared must, a comparison of some interest may be made of the other data.

The free run from the vat is the young wine which flows off without pressure when the vat is tapped, and the press wine is that which is recovered from the pomace on the press. Usually some time elapses between these two operations as is noted in the history of each vat. This element of time would of itself affect the condition of the wine as to the relative alcohol and sugar content, but would not affect the final result in so far as alcohol content is concerned. But the change in total acid content is decidedly important and raises a most serious question as to the practice observed during this investigation. The average acid found in the free run is 0.66 gram per 100 cc, which is not too high for a young wine of the strength and body of the material under consideration. But the press wine gave an average of 0.84 gram acid, which renders such a wine entirely too sour.

While it is true that the proportion of press wine to free run is usually quite small, yet with such a high acid content as here shown its effect on the quality of the wine when mixed with the free run is serious. Note in this instance that the sample of young wine from the cask taken after the wine was almost dry gave 0.739 gram of acid, which is above the limit for good quality in such a wine.

The variation of acid in the several vats only goes to show how important it is to study this constituent in the fruit so as to determine how it is affected by the different soils and exposures, and by the methods of culture.

The comparison of acid content of free run and press wine in the vats run to cask 26, unyeasted, are not so striking as for cask 64, yeasted, but it must be noted that fermentation did not progress to so great a degree of attenuation in the former, and further the acid shown in the first sample from vats 1, 6. and 8 is strikingly low. While the accuracy of these first samples can not be trusted yet as all were taken in the same manner it is evident that the grapes used in the unyeasted vats were decidedly less acid than those in the yeasted vats The volatile acid in every instance shows a good condition as to soundness of the fermentation.

The increase of the sugar-free solids as the fermentation progressed is marked, as was to be expected, and the difference in solids between the wines from the two casks shows also the effect of incomplete fermentation on the pulp in the case of vats 1, 6, and 8.

The pomace samples show a very variable composition as to alcohol, sugar, and acids. It is peculiarly difficult to take a small sample of a grape pomace which shall be a composite of the mass, and this may account for some of the variations. But the very high sugar content of the pomace from vat 1 is due to imperfect fermentation of the pulp. The high acid content of the pomace samples corresponds with the known fact that the free juice, either before or after fermentation, does not carry as much acid as the pulp.

It would appear that a method by which the fermented pulp could be well drained and not submitted to pressure would give a wine of much better character than when the press wine is mixed with the free run.

O

BIBLIOLIFE

Old Books Deserve a New Life
www.bibliolife.com

Did you know that you can get most of our titles in our trademark **EasyScript**™ print format? **EasyScript**™ provides readers with a larger than average typeface, for a reading experience that's easier on the eyes.

Did you know that we have an ever-growing collection of books in many languages?

Order online:
www.bibliolife.com/store

Or to exclusively browse our **EasyScript**™ collection:
www.bibliogrande.com

At BiblioLife, we aim to make knowledge more accessible by making thousands of titles available to you – quickly and affordably.

Contact us:
BiblioLife
PO Box 21206
Charleston, SC 29413

CPSIA information can be obtained
at www.ICGtesting.com
Printed in the USA
LVIC040745071212
3206LVUK00001BA